COMMUNITY PARTICIPATION & INDEPENDENCE SKILLS

LIFE SKILLS WORKBOOK FOR TEENS WITH AUTISM & ASPERGER'S

HAPPY FROG PRESS

Print ISBN 978-1-7752852-8-1

Happy Frog Press

www.HappyFrogPress.com

INTRODUCTION

Welcome to **Community Participation & Independence Skills for Teens with Autism & Asperger's**.

This book is designed to guide you through the process of assessing and teaching your ASD learner the skills they need to successfully navigate a wide variety of experiences in their community.

Like their peers, teens and young adults with Autism and Asperger's often seek more independence as they move into their teens and twenties. However, caregivers are often concerned that their ASD teens do not have the skills to independently navigate outings and activities in the community successfully.

Using the checklists of skills in this book, you will know what what to teach your learner so they can participate successfully in community activities. The thoroughness of the checklists will also allow you, and your teen learner, to have confidence that they can successfully handle a wide variety of experiences.

This book is designed to be practical and hands-on. Key features include:

Checklists Include Foundation Skills + Community Activity Skills

The book focuses on two types of skills that are required for successful outings in the community.

Foundation skills are those skills that are applicable to a wide variety of outings, such as paying for goods, dressing appropriately, and walking safely and confidently. The beginning of the Foundation Skills section contains a master list of the included skills.

In addition to the Foundation skills, the book contains assessment and education goals for twenty-nine individual *Community Activities*. These activities include catching a bus, buying groceries, using an ATM, etc. The beginning of the Community Activities section contains a master list of the included activities.

Skills are Broken Down into Small Steps

Breaking larger goals into smaller steps is a key element in supporting ASD learners. Focusing on one learning step at a time allows for targeted teaching, faster progress and quicker success.

Each foundation skill and community activity in this workbook is broken down into the component skills needed for successful community participation.

For example, catching a bus includes the skills of determining the route, purchasing a ticket, flagging down the bus, choosing a seat, etc.

While some of these skills initially seem simple, you may be surprised by the amount of social knowledge that is needed in order to make successful choices.

When your learner has mastered the component skills for a community activity, you can be confident they have the basic skills required for successful participation.

Prepares Learners for the Unexpected

Many students easily learn the basic skills for participating in community outings. However, it is also extremely important that your learner knows what to do in unexpected situations.

For example, when catching a bus, your learner will need to know what to do if she misses her stop or if she gets off at the wrong stop.

All the community activities and foundation skills in the book include a list of potential problems. Knowing how to handle these issues will increase the confidence of both you and your learner.

Support your learner's steps towards independence by using this book to build a confident and capable teen who is ready to participate in community activities.

SAFETY CONCERNS

Please be aware that venturing out into the community brings additional safety concerns. As the parent, teacher or caregiver of this learner, you are responsible for choosing appropriate independence goals for your student.

Your learner may reach the stage of complete independence - successfully operating in the community alone. Alternatively, perhaps the best goal for your learner is that they can operate without scaffolding in the company of a caregiver.

Your learner's personal safety and capabilities should be a key criteria in determining the level of independence you are aiming for.

Keep in mind that goals can be increased over time. This year your goal may be that your learner can order and pay in a coffee shop while you wait at a table. In a year or two, when your learner is older, you may choose to increase the level of independence.

HOW TO GET STARTED

You can get started in three easy steps.

1. Get to Know the Book
2. Identify Your Initial Priorities
3. Plan Your First Teaching Session

In this section, we will give you a quick overview of what you can find in this book. The following two sections will get you started with supporting your learner towards independence when participating in the community.

ABOUT THIS BOOK

This book is designed as a reference for you to write on, scribble reminders in, note progress, etc. It is your bible to your student's progress to independence - however that might be defined for your learner.

The main sections of the book are:

Foundations Skills Section: Contains skill checklists for developing sixteen foundation skill that are used in many community activities. Foundation skills include activities like paying for an item, walking safely and route-finding skills.

Community Activities Section: This section contains skills checklists for 29 community activities such as catching a bus, going to the movies, etc.

Forms Section: This section contains several Learning Priorities Analysis worksheets for you to use to determine your student's top learning priorities and to plan individual learning sessions. This section also contains a sample assessment scale.

In addition, there are complete lists of the foundation skills and community activities, which you can use as a master list. These master lists precede each individual section as well.

Before You Go Section: A quick guide to additional resources that may be useful for your student.

THE SKILLS CHECKLISTS

Each of the skills checklists contains a list of subtasks or sub skills that are a part of the larger activity.

For example, the 'catching a bus' activity includes more than twelve subtasks such as waiting in line, waiting for people to get off the bus, showing your ticket, choosing a seat or a place to stand, etc.

These skills can be taught individually and allow you to really identify and focus on the subtasks that are more challenging for your learner.

In the checklists, each sub-task contains an area for you to take notes like the following.

☐☐☐☐☐☐☐

Use this area in any way that suits your needs. We often use the boxes to code for current skill level (such as A for Aware, IC for independent with a caregiver, etc).[1] This allows us to see progress over time.

In the white space we make notes of particular challenges, things to do next time, etc.

Keep in mind, this area can used in any way that benefits you supporting your student.

---

1. The next section introduces a method for evaluating current skill level.

IDENTIFY YOUR INITIAL
LEARNING PRIORITIES

As you browse through the book, you will probably encounter many skills that you would like your student to learn. However, to ensure success, it is important to limit the number of goals you are working on at any one time.

We suggest limiting yourself to 3-5 subtasks from one or two preferred activities. For example, if your student wants to learn how to ride a bus and go to the grocery store, your initial goals may look like:

- Walk safely to a specific location (grocery store and bus stop)
- Pay for an item with cash (useful for both targeted activities)
- Ask where to find specific items
- Get on the bus and pay/display ticket

Note, having a goal like 'catching a bus' is not ideal. The activity of catching a bus contains more than a dozen subtasks. This is too many skills to target at once for effective and motivating progress.

We have included a Learning Priorities Analysis worksheet at the back of this book to aid you in identifying your initial learning priorities.

You can photocopy the page, or just write in the book. Alternatively, you can download and print the worksheet from here:

http://www.happyfrogapps.com/community-worksheet

Learning Priorities Analysis Worksheet

Follow these steps to complete the worksheet and identify some starting goals for your student.

1. Choose the Top Three Activities

Browse the book to identify the top three activities your learner (or you) would most like to prioritize.

Write your top three activities in the first section of the worksheet.

As explained above, we encourage you to limit yourself to three community activities so that your actions are more targeted and your learner sees quicker progress.

2. Identify the Necessary Sub-Skills

Now that you have chosen your three activities, consider which foundation skills are required to support those activities.

For example, catching a bus uses the foundation skills such as waiting in line and paying with cash or credit card.

A master list of foundation skills can be found at the front of the Foundation Skills section and in the Forms section.

Choose 3-5 foundation skills that would benefit your learner.

If your learner already has strong skills in the required foundation skills, browse the page for each identified activity to find sub-skills that your learner needs to work on.

For example, to learn how to catch a bus, your learner may need to learn how to top up a pass, how signal for the next stop, how to find an appropriate seat, etc.

3. Assess Your Learner's Current Skill Level

Once you have your list of targeted sub-skills, evaluate your learner's current skill level at this task.

If you don't know the student's current level, you may need to do the activity with the student to ascertain the current competency level.

You can use any rating scale you prefer for assessing competency, but we find the following handy.

Awareness (A): Learner is aware that other people perform this skill but has not done it himself.

Highly Scaffolded (HS): Learner can perform the skill/activity with a high level of scaffolding such as verbal and non-verbal prompts.

Minimally Scaffolded (MS): Learner can perform skill/activity with a minimal amount of scaffolding.

Independent with Caregiver (IC): Learner can perform the skill without prompts or other scaffolding while accompanied by a caregiver. (The caregiver could be seated at a distance, but the learner is aware that there is a caregiver available.)

Independent Solo (IS): The learner completes the activity in the community either by himself or with a peer.

4. Decide on Independence Goals

Next, decide what level of competency you wish your learner to aim for. Please refer to the section on safety when deciding the level of independence appropriate for your student.

Once you have identified a small set of subtasks for your student, know their current competency and the independence goal you are aiming for, you are ready to plan your first teaching session.

PLAN YOUR FIRST
TEACHING SESSION

The key components for a successful teaching session are:

1. Know what you are teaching
2. Know how to teach your learner
3. Have fun

KNOW WHAT YOU ARE TEACHING

For a successful teaching session, you must know what you are teaching, your learner's current skill level and what your immediate goal is.

For example, one of your goals may be for your learner to pay with a credit card. Previously your student has successfully demonstrated paying with a credit card with three or more prompts from you. Your goal this session is for her to complete the task with only 1-2 prompts.

If you haven't already done so, you can use the Learning Priorities Analysis worksheet in the previous section to determine your learner's top skill priorities and the specific sub-tasks needed for those skills.

For any teaching session, focus on 3-5 sub-tasks only. Focusing on specific sub-tasks, which are a smaller part of a bigger independence goal, will allow you to identify and celebrate your learner's success and progress more frequently. If we only look at a bigger goal, we may miss smaller steps forward.

KNOW HOW TO TEACH YOUR LEARNER

Teaching independence skills is no different to teaching any other skills to an ASD learner, except you may be out in the community instead of in your typical learning location.

Strategies and techniques that work for your learner when teaching other skills, are likely to be your best choice for teaching independence skills.

If you are not familiar with your learner, or are looking for new ideas, the following teaching strategies (in no particular order) are likely to be effective.

- Role-playing
- Modeling, including video modelling
- Social stories
- Step-by-step instructions/ Visual cues
- Prompting

Role-playing is where you act out a scene with your student. Role-playing is a great strategy when first teaching a skill. It can be done in your typical learning location and does not need a trip into the community.

Another advantage of role-playing is that you can demonstrate some of the more challenging variants of the sub-skill you are working on. For example, if you are working on the skill of paying with cash, you can role-play what to do when you don't have enough money for the items you want to purchase.

Role-plays also have the advantage that the learner is required to 'think on their feet' to provide appropriate responses.

Allow your learner to practice all roles in a role-play. For example, let them explore being the cashier in the payment scenario. This will allow them to explore concerns they may have that you may not have thought of.

Modeling is where you (or another expert) demonstrate or model the task for your student.

Modeling is an excellent first step when you venture into the community with your learner. With successful role-play experiences, your learner will be more aware of the steps involved in a task and is more likely to be an observant learner when you model.

Social stories are simple descriptions of an everyday social situation, written from the learner's perspective. Many ASD learners are familiar with social stories.

Social stories can be a great first step for teaching community skills. Like role-play, they can set learners up with what to expect and how to react in a variety of different scenarios related to the targeted task.

Step-by-step instructions. Some learners benefit from having a written record of the required steps in a task. Typically ASD learners do well when these steps are very visual.

Prompting is when the teacher gives explicit clues in order to elicit the desired response from a learner. For example, when the student is paying for an item with a credit card, a verbal prompt could be something like, "Now tap your card on the reader."

Prompts can be:

- Verbal (as in the above example)
- Visual (gestures, cue cards, etc)
- Physical (hand-over-hand)

Usually the least intrusive prompt is preferred. These are usually visual prompts.

Prompts are often used with errorless learning. Using errorless learning, the teacher intervenes with a prompt before errors are made.

When using prompts, it is important to have a plan to fade prompts as quickly as possible so your learner does not become prompt dependent. A learner is prompt dependent when they wait for the prompt in order to begin the next step.

Other Strategies to promote success include:

- Talk or show, don't do both at once.
- Keep words to a minimum
- Break talk/show into small pieces. For example, one or two sentences, then show and repeat.
- Make the steps smaller

Most importantly, make sure your learner is motivated to learn this skill. Without motivation, learning and teaching are extremely challenging! When your learner is motivated, amazing things happen.

Get Out There and Have Fun!!

You are now ready to get started. You have specific goals for your learner and are ready to model, scaffold and enjoy the activities that are important to your student.

Celebrate each learning milestone and be proud of the independence skills your learner is building. All learning and progress is cause for celebration, whatever your final destination!

PART ONE

FOUNDATION SKILLS

1. PAYING

Asks the cost of an item if it is not clear

Understands that tax will be added to make the final price

Makes sure he/she has enough money

Keeps items visible until they have been paid for

Cash Payment

Hands over appropriate bills and coins to pay - doesn't hand over too much money (e.g. extra notes)

Waits for change

☐☐☐☐☐☐☐☐☐

Does a quick check of change before moving too far away

☐☐☐☐☐☐☐☐☐

Puts change away safely

☐☐☐☐☐☐☐☐☐

Card Payment

Checks correct amount is showing

☐☐☐☐☐☐☐☐☐

Uses PIN or tap as appropriate

☐☐☐☐☐☐☐☐☐

Puts card away safely

☐☐☐☐☐☐☐☐☐

POTENTIAL PROBLEMS TO HANDLE

Not enough money to pay

PIN doesn't work

Credit card gets rejected

Wrong change is given

2. WAITING IN LINE

Identifies when there is a line-up for a service

Identifies the end of the line and goes there

Waits patiently in line with appropriate social manners/movement

Takes turn at appropriate time

Moves out of the way when done

POTENTIAL PROBLEMS TO HANDLE

Doesn't notice the line and 'barges in'

Someone else barges in

Doesn't notice line moving forward

Person in front doesn't notice line has moved forward

3. WALKING SAFELY

Crosses road at appropriate location

Uses crosswalk safely

Looks both ways before crossing and stays alert while crossing the road

Walks with appropriate posture

Walks with appropriate speed

Walks next to friend/family when appropriate

Avoids personal space of other pedestrians

Keeps sounds and talking to an appropriate volume

Avoids 'talking-to-self' while out

Follows family rules for approaching dogs or other animals

Watches for cars while walking in parking lots

Identifies safe and unsafe locations

Recognizes when a situation is becoming less safe

Chooses a safe route

POTENTIAL PROBLEMS TO HANDLE

The nearest crosswalk for a busy road is three blocks away

You feel like walking with your hands stretched above your head

You feel like singing loudly as you walk along a busy street

A car had to screech to a stop because you crossed unsafely. You can see the driver is really mad.

4. BIKE RIDING

Use this skill checklist for bike riding, scootering, skateboarding, etc.

Wears helmet (if required)

Checks bicycle is safe to ride

Locks/secures bike at destination

Knows when to lock bike

Knows where to lock bike

Uses signals when riding

Demonstrates understanding of the road rules.

Chooses a safe route to avoid busy streets

Knows how to change a flat tire

Carries tube repair and simple tools

POTENTIAL PROBLEMS TO HANDLE

Gets a flat tire and can't change it

Gears break and bike is unrideable

Can't unlock the lock

Can't lock the bike

There is no bike rack in front of the shop you want to go to

5. BRINGING WHAT IS NEEDED

Carries identifying information on all outings

Brings charged phone on all outings

Brings some money on all outings

Can describe what is needed for a specific outing

Prepares and brings what is needed for a specific outing

POTENTIAL PROBLEMS TO HANDLE

Forgets required document for an outing

Forgets to bring money

Forgets to bring phone

6. ESCALATORS & ELEVATORS

Escalators:

Calmly gets on and off escalators

Lines up to get on escalator if crowded

Stands calmly on escalator

Elevators:

Selects appropriate up or down elevator button

Waits for people to get off before getting on

Gives space for people getting off

Waits turn for getting on

Pushes correct button for intended floor

Presses door open button appropriately to help someone get on at the last minute

Gives appropriate personal space in elevator in different situations (more crowded, less crowded)

Watches for correct floor

Uses manners when time to get off crowded elevator

Understands about emergency button in elevator

POTENTIAL PROBLEMS TO HANDLE

Elevator is too crowded to get on

Misses getting off at correct floor

Elevator stops suddenly and doors don't open

7. ASKING FOR DIRECTIONS OR HELP

These skills are designed for dealing with everyday problems that a learner might encounter. Please see the Emergencies section for more urgent situations.

Tries to solve problem independently first

Knows who to ask for help (and who not to)

Asks for help if necessary (in person, via phone, as per family preferences)

Asks follow-up questions if necessary

POTENTIAL PROBLEMS TO HANDLE

First attempt at help does not succeed

Phone battery is dead

Someone else asks for your directions/help

Problem feels too big to handle

8. DRESSING APPROPRIATELY

Choose skills appropriate for your learner.

Clothes are neat and clean

Hair is neat and clean

Has good hygiene

Clothes and shoes are appropriate for destination and time of day.

Wears clothes appropriate for the weather

Wears shoes appropriate for the weather

Wears or carries accessories appropriate for the weather (e.g. gloves in cold weather)

Makeup and jewelry are appropriate for the destination/time of day

POTENTIAL PROBLEMS TO HANDLE

Forgot to bring jacket

Weather changes significantly

Feels inappropriately dressed upon arrival

Left umbrella somewhere

9. EATING IN PUBLIC

Uses cutlery appropriately

Uses napkin

Talks with empty mouth

Doesn't take overly big mouthfuls

Engages in conversation while eating, including initiating topics, staying on topic etc.

Requests and passes food politely

Takes reasonable portion of shared dishes

Waits for others to finish before leaving table

POTENTIAL PROBLEMS TO HANDLE

Dislikes available food

Doesn't like what he ordered

10. PHONE SKILLS

Calls parent or guardian

Answers phone calls from known people

Follows family rules for answering phone calls from unknown people

Appropriately begins and ends phone calls

Conveys intended message in phone call, even when stressed

Appropriately answers questions asked in a phone call, even when stressed

☐☐☐☐☐☐☐☐

Leaves voicemail messages when necessary

☐☐☐☐☐☐☐☐

Notices he has a voicemail

☐☐☐☐☐☐☐☐

Retrieves voicemail and appropriately saves or deletes

☐☐☐☐☐☐☐☐

Looks up a number from contact list

☐☐☐☐☐☐☐☐

Adds a new contact to contact list

☐☐☐☐☐☐☐☐

Sends texts

☐☐☐☐☐☐☐☐

Receives texts

☐☐☐☐☐☐☐☐

Responds to texts from known people

☐☐☐☐☐☐☐☐

Follows family rules for responding to texts from unknown people

☐☐☐☐☐☐☐☐

Appropriately asks and answers questions via text

☐☐☐☐☐☐☐☐

POTENTIAL PROBLEMS TO HANDLE

Receives inappropriate text or phone call

11. SOCIAL MANNERS

Engages appropriately when encountering close friends or relatives on the street or in a shop.

Engages appropriately when encountering known members of the community on the street or in a shop.

Returns greetings appropriately

Responds with a nod or smile when appropriate

Says "Excuse me" when needed for accidental bumps or requests to get by.

Respects personal space

Holds doors for others when appropriate

Stays out of private areas of shops or other community buildings. Uses correct exits.

Handles delays or other problems and inconveniences calmly

Understands that problems may be caused by other people unintentionally

Covers cough or sneeze

Responds appropriately when introduced to someone

Introduces friends and family to others when appropriate

POTENTIAL PROBLEMS TO HANDLE

Can't remember someone's name

Knows someone but can't figure out who they are

Someone you don't know tries to talk to you

Someone bumps into you and doesn't apologize

Someone you know doesn't notice you

Someone you know ignores you

12. SAFETY/SECURITY

These skills are extremely important for teens who might venture out alone.

Responds appropriately to authority figures

Only shows or tells personal identification to appropriate people

Engages minimally with unknown people

Ignores inappropriate requests from known or unknown people

Reports inappropriate requests to parents or caregiver.

Tells parents of any unusual or problematic encounters

Exits situations where inappropriate behavior is encouraged or encountered

Uses public washroom appropriately

Carries appropriate amount of cash (not too much)

Keeps money and cards safe and unobtrusive

Identifies potentially unsafe situations (loud people, angry people, dark alleys, protests, etc)

Is aware of safety of surroundings and chooses safer options

☐☐☐☐☐☐☐☐

Can recite two emergency contact names and numbers

☐☐☐☐☐☐☐☐

Identifies who to call if he needs help

☐☐☐☐☐☐☐☐

Makes plans only with people he knows and trusts (and who have parent approval)

☐☐☐☐☐☐☐☐

Identifies when people are trying to manipulate him or her

☐☐☐☐☐☐☐☐

Responds appropriately when people are trying to manipulate him/her

☐☐☐☐☐☐☐☐

POTENTIAL PROBLEMS TO HANDLE

Known or unknown person tries to intimidate you into doing something

Known or unknown person harasses you

A group of boys who don't look safe approach you

13. SELF-ADVOCACY / PROBLEM SOLVING

Recognizes when self-advocacy is needed

Remains calm while trying to solve the problem

Explains problem or concern to person who can help

Asks for clarification if needed

Shows confidence

POTENTIAL PROBLEMS TO HANDLE

The first person you ask can't help

The person doesn't understand you

The person gives a solution that you think is wrong

14. ROUTE-FINDING SKILLS

Can read a map or use a GPS to figure out where to go

Can use both electronic and printed maps

Can figure out how to get somewhere using a map or GPS

Can figure out route for multi-leg journeys (e.g. changing bus and/or train)

Can figure out how long to get to a location

Can determine likely arrival time

POTENTIAL PROBLEMS TO HANDLE

You can't figure out which bus to take home.

Your phone dies and you don't remember what bus to take.

The bus you are waiting for doesn't arrive.

You are looking for a particular classroom, but you don't know where it is.

15. TECHNOLOGY

Logs into wifi if available in public places

Asks for wifi network/password from staff

Uses ear buds or headphones to avoid playing loud music/sounds in public places

Keeps phone charged enough for duration of outings

POTENTIAL PROBLEMS TO HANDLE

Phone dies in the middle of your outing

16. EMERGENCIES

Can describe what to do in case of various natural disasters while out (Make the disasters relevant to your location)

Can describe what to do if he/she feels a little unwell while out

Can describe what to do if he/she feels very sick while out

Can describe what to do if he/she is in a car or bus accident

Can describe what to do if he/she witnesses a car or bus accident (with and without other people around)

Can describe what to do if he/she sees someone who is sick or hurt. (Various options to consider - dangerous and non-dangerous situations, many people around versus no people around, known or unknown person involved, etc)

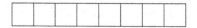

17. PERSONAL CHALLENGES

Your student may have challenges that are unique to him/her. For example, perhaps the sound of a crying baby agitates your learner. In this case, your learner needs appropriate coping mechanisms if this were to happen while he was out. Use these pages to work on skills specific to your learner's needs.

1.

2.

3.

4.

5.

6.

7.

8.

9.

10.

11.

12.

PART TWO

COMMUNITY ACTIVITIES

1. GROCERY STORE

Makes shopping list ahead of time

☐☐☐☐☐☐☐☐☐

Takes a basket or a shopping cart

☐☐☐☐☐☐☐☐☐

Uses basket or cart appropriately (doesn't bump into other people or get in their way)

☐☐☐☐☐☐☐☐☐

Chooses items

☐☐☐☐☐☐☐☐☐

Reads shop signs to find items

☐☐☐☐☐☐☐☐☐

Asks for help in finding items

Waits turn and requests items from bakery/deli/meat department staff

Lines up for the checkout

Uses self-checkout

Engages in appropriate small-talk with cashier. (No requirement to initiate small-talk unless it is culturally required)

Answers questions from the cashier

Packs own groceries with appropriate speed (if required)

Pays with cash or card

Waits for change and does quick check

Shows points card, if appropriate

Takes receipt and groceries

POTENTIAL PROBLEMS TO HANDLE

Not enough money

An item is damaged

Bag is packed too full

Bags are too heavy to carry

Problem with self-checkout machine

Don't know how to scan an item at the self-checkout

Don't understand a question from the cashier

Can't find what you are looking for

2. CATCHING THE BUS

This section covers all the skills required to catch a bus. Work on those which your learner needs to successfully navigate his community.

Knows which bus to catch for a variety of destinations

Locates the bus stop - when going from home and from other locations

Buys ticket or pass

Adds credit to pass

Flags down bus if required

Waits turn to get on the bus

Gets on the correct bus and shows/scans ticket

Keeps ticket safe

Chooses to sit/stand in an appropriate place (may change depending on crowdedness)

Demonstrates appropriate social rules while on the bus

Knows when intended stop is coming

Signals for stop

Gets off the bus appropriately

POTENTIAL PROBLEMS

Missed bus

Missed stop

Lost ticket/pass

Got on wrong bus

Got off at wrong stop

Elderly person gets on the bus with no available seats

Rowdy passenger nearby

Someone you don't know tries talking to you

3. CATCHING THE TRAIN/METRO

If your learner accesses the metro, here are the skills to work on.

Locates the train station

Buys a ticket

Determines which train or trains to catch for various destinations, both familiar and unfamiliar

Finds the correct platform

Shows ticket or goes through automatic gate

Keeps ticket safe

☐☐☐☐☐☐☐☐

Waits appropriately and safely on the platform

☐☐☐☐☐☐☐☐

Waits for people to get off the train

☐☐☐☐☐☐☐☐

Chooses an appropriate place to sit or stand on the train

☐☐☐☐☐☐☐☐

Knows what stop to get off at

☐☐☐☐☐☐☐☐

Demonstrates appropriate social rules while on the train

☐☐☐☐☐☐☐☐

Changes trains to reach destination

☐☐☐☐☐☐☐☐

POTENTIAL PROBLEMS

Missed train

Missed stop

Lost ticket/pass

Got on wrong train

Got off at wrong stop

Elderly person gets on the train with no available seats

Rowdy passenger nearby

4. USING A TAXI/UBER

Select those skills which are relevant for your learner's needs. Not all may be needed.

Orders a taxi using a phone or app

Hails a taxi on a street - recognizes available and unavailable taxis

Knows how to find a taxi stand and wait appropriately

Confirms correct taxi when it arrives

Communicates destination to the driver

Maintains social manners during the drive

Pays at the end with appropriate tip

Adheres to family safety rules for traveling by taxi. (May include choosing official taxi company only, checking for driver ID, etc).

POTENTIAL PROBLEMS

Can't get a taxi

Taxi driver doesn't speak your language

Taxi driver wants to talk and you don't

5. BUYING CLOTHES

These skills can be adapted to other shopping needs such as buying items for school, hobbies, etc.

Knows when to buy new clothes

Chooses an appropriate shop

Knows own size for shirts, pants, shoes

Selects appropriate choices to try on

Responds to questions or comments from sales staff

Requests information from sales staff if needed

Limits number of items to try on to meet store requirements

Finds change room

Locks change room

Tries on clothes and makes final choice

Follows rules for trying on underwear and swim suits

Only comes out of change room when appropriately dressed

Puts un-needed clothes in appropriate location

Takes preferred clothes to checkout

Checks prices are affordable

Pays with cash or card

Keeps receipt

POTENTIAL PROBLEMS TO HANDLE

Cashier suggests signing up for credit card

Not enough money to pay

6. SHOE STORE

Browses shoes and identifies preferred style

Checks price is affordable

Knows or can measure own shoe size

Can describe style of shoe he/she needs to sales staff

Finds correctly sized shoe if other shoe sizes are present on the shelves for customer to self-serve

Asks attendant for the correct size when other sizes are not present

Tries on the shoes and tests them

Asks for a different size if necessary

Pays with cash or card

Keeps receipt

POTENTIAL PROBLEMS TO HANDLE

Correct size is unavailable

Shoes are not comfortable and you don't want to buy them

Shoes are too expensive

7. OTHER TYPES OF STORES

Use this skill list for stores such as a corner store, pet store, sporting good store, etc.

Takes a shopping basket if appropriate

Uses basket appropriately (doesn't bump into other people or get in their way)

Chooses items

Reads shop signs to find items

Asks for help in finding items

Keeps items in view until purchase

Lines up for the checkout

Engages in appropriate small-talk with cashier.

Answers shopping-related questions from the cashier

Pays with cash or card

Waits for change and does quick check

Shows points card or uses gift card, if appropriate

Takes receipt and bought items

POTENTIAL PROBLEMS TO HANDLE

Not enough money

An item is damaged

Bag is packed too full

Bags are too heavy to carry

Problem with self-checkout machine

Don't know how to scan an item at the self-checkout

Don't understand a question from the cashier

Can't find what you are looking for

8. BUYING AND GIVING A BIRTHDAY GIFT

This checklist can also be used for other gift-giving occasions, such as Christmas.

Intended recipient is an appropriate choice

Budgets an appropriate amount for the gift

Thinks about what the recipient would like

Decides where to go to buy the gift

Buys gift (and wrapping paper/card if needed)

Wraps present and writes on card

Gives gift appropriately

Accepts thanks appropriately

POTENTIAL PROBLEMS TO HANDLE

Preferred gift is too expensive

Can't find the ideal gift

Gift is too large to wrap

9. COFFEE SHOP

Use this skill list in any casual dining environment. Specific skills for fast food restaurants can be found in the next section.

Reads the menu

Waits in line

Decides what he wants before reaching the front of the line

Understands the drink sizes and how to order

Answers barista's questions about his order

Decides quickly on an alternative when first choice is not available

Has payment ready

Picks up drink when it is available

Finds a place to sit

Maintains social manners while in the coffee shop

Cleans up after himself

Asks for washroom key if needed

Takes all his belongings when he leaves

POTENTIAL PROBLEMS TO HANDLE

Accidentally spills drink

Accidentally takes wrong drink

Not enough money to pay

10. FAST FOOD RESTAURANT

Reviews menu and makes choice before approaching counter

Waits in line to order food

Places order clearly and concisely

Responds to questions about the order

Pays with cash or card

Waits in an appropriate location for food

Recognizes when order is ready

Carries food to the table

Gets required utensils and condiments

Eats without disturbing other customers

Clears table and sorts trash as appropriate

POTENTIAL PROBLEMS TO HANDLE

Not enough money

Preferred choice is not available

Wrong food came in order

Missed hearing your name/number

11. SIT-DOWN RESTAURANT

Use this skill list for any restaurant where the waiter comes to the table.

Checks in with the host/hostess

Waits for a table

Chooses food and drink in a reasonable time frame

Asks questions if necessary

Gives order clearly and concisely to waiter

Describes allergy information clearly

☐☐☐☐☐☐☐☐☐

Answers waiter's questions about options

☐☐☐☐☐☐☐☐☐

Gets waiter's attention if needed

☐☐☐☐☐☐☐☐☐

Asks for the bill

☐☐☐☐☐☐☐☐☐

Checks bill for accuracy

☐☐☐☐☐☐☐☐☐

Calculates tip

☐☐☐☐☐☐☐☐☐

Pays with cash or card

☐☐☐☐☐☐☐☐☐

POTENTIAL PROBLEMS TO HANDLE

Wrong food is delivered to the table

Food takes an excessively long time to come

Bill is incorrect

Something ordered is forgotten

12. GOING TO THE DOCTOR

Select the skills appropriate for your learner.

Makes a doctors appointment

Gets to the appointment on time

Brings any required paperwork (e.g. insurance details)

Checks in with the receptionist

Waits appropriately in the waiting room

Responds when name is called

Explains reason for visit

Answers doctor's questions

Listens to the doctor's instructions (or asks for them to be written down)

Pays

Puts receipt and prescription in a safe place

POTENTIAL PROBLEMS TO HANDLE

Late for the appointment

Don't understand what the doctor says

Don't know the answer to some of the doctor's questions

13. GOING TO THE DENTIST

Select the skills appropriate for your learner. If necessary, you can adapt these skills for visits to other medical practitioners such as physiotherapists, naturopaths, etc.

Makes a dentist appointment

Cleans teeth before appointment

Gets to the appointment on time

Brings any required paperwork (e.g. insurance details)

Checks in with the receptionist

Waits appropriately in the waiting room

☐☐☐☐☐☐☐☐

Sits calmly in the chair during the appointment

☐☐☐☐☐☐☐☐

Explains reason for visit

☐☐☐☐☐☐☐☐

Answers dentist's questions

☐☐☐☐☐☐☐☐

Listens to the dentists's instructions (or asks for them to be written down)

☐☐☐☐☐☐☐☐

Pays with cash or card

☐☐☐☐☐☐☐☐

Keeps receipt and gives it to parents

POTENTIAL PROBLEMS TO HANDLE

Late for the appointment

Forgot insurance details

14. FILLING A PRESCRIPTION

Depending on your country, some details may differ. Alter the skills to suit your learner's needs.

Goes to local pharmacy

Waits in line to drop off prescription

Answers pharmacist's questions

Asks how long until the prescription is ready

Waits appropriate amount of time

Picks up the medication

Listens to the pharmacist's directions

Gives insurance details if needed

Pays

Puts medication away safely

POTENTIAL PROBLEMS TO HANDLE

Don't know the answer to some of the pharmacist's questions

Don't understand what the pharmacist says

15. BANKING - ATM

Choose the ATM banking skills which are appropriate for your learner at this point in their journey.

Remembers PIN and keeps it safe

Protects PIN number from view

Withdraws money from an ATM

Deposits money at an ATM

Deposits a check at an ATM

Checks balance at the ATM

Puts card and money away safely

Checks ATM for safety before using

POTENTIAL PROBLEMS TO HANDLE

Forgets PIN

Not enough money in the account

ATM is not open

ATM is not working

ATM area does not feel safe

16. BANKING - AT THE COUNTER

These skills are for students who need to access banking services from a teller.

Waits in line for a teller

States request clearly and concisely

Shows ID or enters PIN if requested

Deposits a check

Deposits money

Withdraws money with a teller

Asks a question about her account

Puts away cards and money safely

POTENTIAL PROBLEMS TO HANDLE

Forgets PIN

Not enough money in the account

Doesn't have the correct ID

17. HAIR SALON

This skill list can be used for any type of salon, such as hair, nail, waxing, etc.

Makes an appointment

Gets to appointment on time

Waits until he/she is called

Tells the hair stylist what he/she wants

Answers questions about hair style

Does appropriate small-talk with stylist

Maintains appropriate body movement while hair is being cut/styled

Provides socially appropriate feedback to the stylist when done

Pays with card or cash

Adds appropriate tip

POTENTIAL PROBLEMS TO HANDLE

Not enough money

Stylist misinterpreted instructions

18. LIBRARY

Looks up books in catalogue to find location

Finds books on shelves based on location number

Can find books in different parts of the library (Adult, Young Adult, Children's section), if needed

Reviews books before choosing

Keeps number of books within allowed limit

Asks for help in finding books, if necessary

Borrow books using automatic checkout or librarian

Pays overdue fines

Returns books by due date

POTENTIAL PROBLEMS TO HANDLE

Lost library card

Overdue fine

Haven't got a library card

Forgot library card at home

Can't find book

Don't know how to use the catalogue

19. POST OFFICE

Waits in line for turn

☐☐☐☐☐☐☐☐☐

Explains what service is needed to the cashier clearly and concisely.

☐☐☐☐☐☐☐☐☐

Picks up package

☐☐☐☐☐☐☐☐☐

Posts package or letters

☐☐☐☐☐☐☐☐☐

Buys stamps

☐☐☐☐☐☐☐☐☐

Answer cashier's questions

Asks questions if needed

Pays

Checks mailbox

POTENTIAL PROBLEMS TO HANDLE

Don't have appropriate ID

Don't have enough money

Received letter/package is not for you

20. HANGING OUT AT THE MALL

Stays in public area of mall

Spends a reasonable amount of time browsing in a store when no purchase is planned

Demonstrates social manners when in public places

Keeps away from unsafe places or people

POTENTIAL PROBLEMS TO HANDLE

Security guard asks you to move on

You are approached by an unfriendly peer

You are approached by an adult you don't know

Someone with a clipboard wants to ask you some questions

Someone says they have something to show you outside

21. TAKING THE DOG FOR A WALK

Follows leash laws

Keeps dog under control

Uses appropriate social manners with other dog walkers and/or other pedestrians

Keeps dog off private property

Takes materials to scoop poop if needed

Scoops poop if needed

POTENTIAL PROBLEMS TO HANDLE

Aggressive dog approaches your dog

Your dog acts aggressively to someone else or another dog

Your dog bites someone

Another dog bites you or your dog

22. HANGING OUT AT THE COMMUNITY YOUTH CENTER

With a few adjustments, this skill set could also be used for hanging out at an arcade or similar location.

Uses appropriate social manners upon arrival

Takes turns using the games and equipment

Responds to requests from youth center staff

Responds to friendly overtures from other teens/young adults

Responds appropriately to requests from other teens/young adults

Doesn't hog a preferred game

Uses social manners during the time at the center

Asks to join appropriately

Takes leave appropriately

POTENTIAL PROBLEMS TO HANDLE

No one wants to join in playing with you

Another teen is hassling you or bugging you

You don't want to stay but your mom isn't picking you up for an hour

23. USING COMMUNITY SPORTS FIELDS/COURTS/SKATE PARK

Shares space with other people who want to use the space

☐☐☐☐☐☐☐☐

Avoids getting in other people's way in shared spaces like skateparks

☐☐☐☐☐☐☐☐

Handles when other people get in his/her way in shared spaces like skateparks

☐☐☐☐☐☐☐☐

Maintains social manners while in public

☐☐☐☐☐☐☐☐

Avoids bothering other people in the area with noise/loose balls, etc

☐☐☐☐☐☐☐☐

Follows local rules for time using space (e.g. some locales have a 30 minutes limit on using a public tennis court when someone is waiting)

POTENTIAL PROBLEMS TO HANDLE

A group of people don't leave the court when their time is up

You don't know the local rules for using a space and other people look like they want to use the space

The people on the next court are swearing loudly

Some little kids get in the way at the skate park

Some older teens get in the way at the skate park

24. GOING TO THE MOVIES OR A CONCERT

Buys tickets ahead of time or at the venue, as appropriate

Purchases snacks

Shows ticket to staff when requested

Finds correct theatre and/or finds correct seats, if seating is assigned

Lets other people get past to further seats

Maintains social norms while watching the movie/concert

Exits appropriately at the end of the event

POTENTIAL PROBLEMS TO HANDLE

Don't know which theatre to go to

Can't find designated seat

People behind you are talking loudly through the movie

You need to use the bathroom in the middle of the movie/concert

25. GOING TO THE GYM

Takes needed gear to gym

Checks in on arrival

Pays with credit card or cash — or shows valid membership card to front desk staff

Gets changed

Keeps own belongings organized

Puts belongings in a safe location

Signs up for equipment if there is a sign-up sheet

Arrives on time for assigned turn

Takes turns on busy equipment

Returns equipment to its proper location

Wipes down equipment after use

Uses headphones if listening to music

Adheres to gym rules for time spent on equipment

Asks gym staff questions, if needed

Returns social smiles and nods or small talk from other gym participants

Maintains social manners during gym visit

POTENTIAL PROBLEMS TO HANDLE

Don't know where to put belongings

Don't know how to use a specific piece of equipment

Don't know how to sign-up for rowing machine

Some people are hogging the free weights

26. ATTENDING A COMMUNITY CLASS

Use this skills checklist for community classes such as dance, martial arts, art, yoga, etc.

Arrives on time

Brings needed equipment

Chooses appropriate location to sit/stand

Exchanges friendly greetings with classmates when appropriate

Exchanges small talk with classmates, if appropriate

Attends to the teacher during class

Follows instructions during class

Maintains social manner during class

Leaves appropriately

POTENTIAL PROBLEMS TO HANDLE

Classroom has changed to a different location

There is a substitute teacher

You arrive after class starts

Someone is sitting where you like to sit

You forgot to do the homework/practice.

There is a test today and you forgot

27. HANGING OUT WITH FRIENDS

Makes plans to hang out with friends

Chooses appropriate place to meet with friends

Chooses appropriate activity to do with friends

Arrives on time

Greets friends appropriately

Maintains social manners while out with friends

Initiates topics when talking with friends

Stays on topic when talking with friends

Responds to friend's topics

Indicates when he is ready to leave

Leaves appropriately

POTENTIAL PROBLEMS TO HANDLE

Friends don't arrive

Planned activity is not available

You are running late

You are running late and you forgot your phone

You didn't bring enough money

Someone you don't like joins the group

Some unfriendly peers bother you and your friends

29. VISITING A FRIEND'S HOUSE

Greets host when he/she arrives

If appropriate, greets friend's parents when he/she arrives

Follows family rules about what houses he is allowed to go to

Follows family rules about whether a responsible adult must be present

Shows appropriate social manners while at his friend's house

Thanks friend (and parents) before leaving

POTENTIAL PROBLEMS TO HANDLE

You forget your friend's parents' names

Your friend's little brother is being really annoying

Your friend's older sister suggests you do something inappropriate

You are served food you can't eat

29. ATTENDING A PARTY AT A PRIVATE HOUSE

As always, use your judgement about which skills are appropriate for your teen, especially with this section.

Follows family rules about whether he/she is allowed to be at a party at a friend's house

Says no to illegal substances such as alcohol or drugs

Makes good choices about what are safe drinks

Gets own drink and does not leave it unattended

Makes safe choices about who to hang out with

Makes safe choices about what activities/games to engage in

Knows how to leave a party if he/she feels unsafe

POTENTIAL PROBLEMS TO HANDLE

You don't know anyone except your friend, and he is busy

There is someone you would like to meet

You are bored at the party

You don't know what to do at the party

There are lots of drunk people at the party

You feel unsafe at the party

You think you might have eaten or drank something unsafe

Your friend wants to go somewhere else

30. PERSONAL CHOICE

This section is for adding any community activity not included in the book.

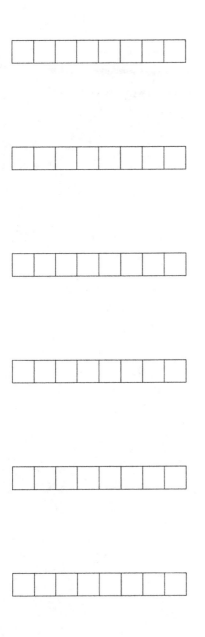

PART THREE

FORMS & MASTER LISTS

Priorities Worksheet

Top 3 Activities	Current Capability	Goal

Required Foundation Skills	Current Capability	Goal

Initial Skill Priorities

Priorities Worksheet

Top 3 Activities	Current Capability	Goal

Required Foundation Skills	Current Capability	Goal

Initial Skill Priorities

Priorities Worksheet

Top 3 Activities	Current Capability	Goal

Required Foundation Skills	Current Capability	Goal

Initial Skill Priorities

Priorities Worksheet

Top 3 Activities	Current Capability	Goal

Required Foundation Skills	Current Capability	Goal

Initial Skill Priorities

Priorities Worksheet

Top 3 Activities	Current Capability	Goal

Required Foundation Skills	Current Capability	Goal

Initial Skill Priorities

1. Paying with cash or card
2. Waiting in Line
3. Walking Safely
4. Bike Riding
5. Bringing What is Needed
6. Escalators & Elevators
7. Asking for Directions or Help
8. Dressing Appropriately
9. Eating in Public
10. Phone Skills
11. Social Manners
12. Security/Safety
13. Self Advocacy
14. Route-Finding Skills
15. Technology
16. Emergencies
17. Personal Challenges

COMMUNITY ACTIVITY MASTER LIST

1. Grocery Store
2. Catching the Bus
3. Catching the Train/Metro
4. Taxi/Uber
5. Buying Clothes
6. Shoe Store
7. Other Types of Stores
8. Buying and Giving a Birthday Gift
9. Coffee Shop
10. Fast-Food Restaurant
11. Sit-Down Restaurant
12. Doctor's Office
13. Dentist Visit
14. Filling a Prescription
15. Banking - ATM
16. Banking - At the Counter
17. Hair Salon
18. Library
19. Post Office
20. Hanging Out at the Mall
21. Taking the Dog for a Walk
22. Hanging Out at the Community Youth Group
23. Using Community Sports Fields, Courts & Skate Parks
24. Going to the Movies or a Concert
25. Going to the Gym
26. Attending a Community Class
27. Hanging Out with Friends
28. Visiting a Friend's House
29. Attending a Party at a Private House

SAMPLE EVALUATION/INDEPENDENCE CRITERIA

Awareness (A):

Learner is aware that other people perform this skill but has not done it himself.

Highly Scaffolded (HS):

Learner can perform the skill/activity with a high level of scaffolding such as verbal or non-verbal prompts.

Minimally Scaffolded (MS):

Learner can perform skill/activity with minimal amount of scaffolding.

Independent with Caregiver (IC):

Learner can perform the skill without prompts or other scaffolding while accompanied by a caregiver. (The caregiver could be seated at a distance, but the learner is aware that there is a caregiver available.)

Independent Solo (IS):

The learner completes the activity in the community either by himself or with a peer.

BEFORE YOU GO

If you found this book useful, please leave a short review on Amazon. It makes an amazing difference for independent publishers like Happy Frog Press. Just two sentences will do!

Don't forget to look for other workbooks from Happy Frog Press, such as the **Six-Minute Thinking Skills** series, publishing in 2018 & 2019.

Your learners might also benefit from our **Six-Minute Social Skills series**.

The workbooks in this series build core social skills for kids who have social skills challenges, such as those with Autism, Asperger's and ADHD.

Although numbered, these books can be used in any order.

CERTIFICATE
OF
ACHIEVEMENT

THIS CERTIFICATE IS AWARDED TO

_____

IN RECOGNITION OF

_____

_____   _____

DATE   SIGNATURE